FIND THE MAGIC IN YOU:

EXPERIENCE YOUR EVOLUTION

Felice Izzarelli

TABLE OF CONTENTS

INTRODUCTION

HOW TO USE THIS BOOK FOR YOUR HIGHEST GOOD

When you start your day, choose a chakra that you would like to work with that day and read the section in this book about that chakra. Do a 5 to 20 minute meditation using the vowel sounds, or mantra to align that chakra with your universal vibration. Then, recite the associated affirmation three times. Write it down on a piece of paper to carry with you and repeat it throughout your day.

Next you would move down the page and look at the animals. You could be thinking of the task which is in front of you, or a situation on which you need some guidance. Let your 'gut feelings' or 'guidance' direct you to choose which animal is for you today. You will be surprised at the answer. You will be carrying that energy with you throughout the day.

Finally, look at the stones. Find the stone which matches the animal you've chosen and read that affirmation. The combination of all three will be the ingredients of your reconnection healing meditation for the day.

This is your journey. You are the creator of your world. When you learn how to tap into the vibrations of the universe you will have everything you will ever need, because the key to the magic is within you.

For more information on upcoming books for the intermediate student and the advanced student, meditation CDs and ongoing classes, go to www.experientialevolution.com.

Felice Izzarelli

CHAPTER ONE

WHAT IS A MANTRA?

A Mantra is really nothing more than a form of prayer. Each center in the chakra system has its own vibration. The universe is made of vibration, the world is made of vibration, and we are made of vibration. Mantras are used to help us tap into different frequencies of the universe. We use different sounds to raise the vibrations within ourselves as we tap into our higher consciousness. Each of the seven chakras is assigned its own note and sound, and we use these to help us awaken the chakra centers within each of us.

There are two ways to work with these vibrations:

The first is to make the sound of the mantra, for example, lam, the root chakra mantra. Take a deep breath and visualize the breath going all the way to your base chakra. Then as you exhale, say the prayer or mantra-word 'lam' as you visualize your root chakra being activated. Visualize that energy rising up within your body to your crown chakra. Do this for fifteen to twenty minutes a day.

For the second method it may be helpful to record the different musical notes assigned to each chakra, and then listen to the appropriate note as you visualize the chakra and animal that you have chosen to work with. Take a deep breath and visualize the breath going all the way to your base chakra. Then, as you exhale, see the energy rising up within your body to your crown chakra. Do this for fifteen to twenty minutes a day.

CHAPTER TWO

WHAT ARE CHAKARAS?

Chakras are energy centers in your body. They are the points of life-energy that lie within each of us: our life force. Every living thing on this planet has a life force. There are seven chakras, and each chakra has its own color and energy.

Once we learn how to tap into these different energies, or chakras, we can take an active and conscious role in our spiritual journey. Each chakra has a different sound and note to help us unlock the universal energy within each of us. As we work with each chakra, we release old energy and replace it with a vibrant universal energy that helps us to move forward in our spiritual quest.

We all are passing through one of the most important phases in existence; it's called life, and it is a great period of growth. Each trial you encounter and conquer will add to your soul's growth.

As we grow spiritually, we gain insight and understanding into the purpose of all things. We already have the tools we'll need for every experience and for every lesson life brings to us. We have come to this earth-plane for our soul's journey to our higher selves.

Longing for something better is not enough; one must make an effort: slowly, steadily, living each day better than the last. We must learn to look at life with a spiritual eye and discover the lessons that are needed for our individual and spiritual growth. Working with the chakras, their notes and sounds, we reveal a map to self empowerment. This map is our guide as we journey within to seek our higher consciousness.

CHAPTER THREE

A JOURNEY OF ONE'S CHAKARAS

This chapter will guide you through the basics of the chakras. There are seven chakras in your body, and each offers a different challenge and opportunity in self-discovery and growth. Each has a particular emotional and spiritual purpose, and each offers a lesson to be learned. Here we will cover the individual chakras and their characteristics.

The First Chakra – The Root Chakra

The root chakra is located at the base of the spine, and its color is red. The kundalini wraps 3 ½ times around this first chakra. The root chakra is of the material world and concerns grounding oneself and one's ability to survive. Signs of an imbalanced chakra are feelings of weakness, of being alone, and of having low energy. When the root chakra is healthy and balanced, one feels energized and has the energy to complete one's tasks and to stand up for oneself. One will feel a zest for life and know feelings of trust and security.

The note for the root chakra is C, its tone is U, its element is earth, its instrument is the drum, and its mantra is lam.

To help achieve a balanced chakra one might wear red or eat red foods, perhaps an apple.

A helpful exercise: Say the mantra lam using the beat of a drum, and focus on grounding oneself. Visualize a red ball of light at the base of your spine; see it grow brighter and brighter within.

Affirmation: I am supported and safe in the universe.

The Second Chakra – The Sacral Chakra

The sacral chakra is located two inches below the navel, and its color is orange. The sacral chakra's focus is on bringing balance into ones life; the yin and yang, movement and flow. The sacral chakra concerns ones sexuality, relationships, and friendships.

Signs of an imbalanced chakra may be relationship issues, difficulty with making decisions, or problems getting along with others. This imbalance may also manifest itself in feelings of helplessness or of being victimized.

When the sacral chakra is healthy and balanced, one has the ability to express ones desires and to find love and trust in relationships. One will see that everything in life is a choice, and that we are all responsible for our own happiness, or unhappiness.

The note for the sacral chakra is D, its tone is O, its element is water, its instrument is the flute, and its mantra is va.

A helpful exercise: Say the mantra va while visualizing the color orange; see the color growing brighter and brighter within you.

Affirmation: I am responsible for my own happiness, or unhappiness.

The Third Chakra – The Solar Plexus Chakra

The solar plexus chakra is located two inches above the navel, and its color is yellow. Its focus is to awaken the power within, and to help one tap into one's feelings. It is where healing begins within oneself, and where one's feelings are awakened. It is the center that brings into balance the upper and lower chakras.

If this chakra is blocked, one may have feelings of being put upon, or become power hungry and believe that one is always right. An attitude of 'do unto others before they can do unto you' may develop.

When the solar plexus chakra is healthy and balanced, it gives one feelings of balance and energy, of harmony and flexibility. One may become motivated, and in turn be able to motivate others. One will come to understand that each of us is in charge of our own life, responsible for creating our own reality.

The note for the solar plexus chakra is E, its tone is ah, its element is fire, its instrument is any stringed instrument, and its mantra is ram.

Along with any stringed instrument, laughter is very helpful in awakening this chakra.

Affirmation: I create my own reality.

The Fourth Chakra – The Heart Chakra

The heart chakra is located in the center of the chest, and its color is green. The heart chakra concerns the opening of one's heart to the spirit and to the softness of love. It is where one can open oneself to the heavens and feel the joy of life and the peace within. When this chakra is blocked, one may feel that things have stopped in life or may experience feelings of loneliness or a lack of forgiveness for oneself and for others. There may be a low level of love-flow in one's life.

An open heart chakra allows one to feel the universe opening up, and to realize that one is opening up to one's own universe within. Things change around us as we change the vibrations within. When one works to balance the heart chakra, one will experience feelings of physical lightness and a sense of well-being. One will gain awareness of one's soul and of the flow of unconditional love. With this will come the ability to love and to receive love.

The note for the heart chakra is F, its tone is A, its element is air, its instrument is the bell, and its mantra is ya.

Affirmation: All is well my world today.

I know love and joy for myself and for all those whom are around me.

The Fifth Chakra – The Throat Chakra

The throat chakra is located in the middle of the throat. Its color is blue. The throat chakra is where we have vibrations of what we are feeling. This chakra concerns our understanding the power of the spoken word. From this chakra we send out vibrations; vibrations have meaning to them, and each of us is responsible for the vibrations we put forth when speaking. The throat chakra helps us to be aware of which chakra centers we are coming from.

When this chakra is blocked, one may experience a sore throat or be unable to speak one's truth. One may have a poor self-image, or a sense that the universe is an unfriendly or unsafe place to be. When the throat chakra is healthy and balanced, it allows one to express oneself with clarity and communicate effectively with others. It gives one a feeling of peace.

One's creativity will blossom and one will be able to share ideas with others and feel respect for the ideas of others. One will be able to express one's true nature and understand and accept one's purpose in life.

The note for the throat chakra is G, its tone is I, its element is sound, its instrument is the bamboo flute, and its mantra is ha.

Affirmation: All is well my world today.

I know love and joy for myself and for all those whom are around me.

The Sixth Chakra – The Brow Chakra

The brow chakra is located between the eyes, and its color is indigo. This chakra is sometimes referred to as the third eye, and it is considered the circle of light. It gives one insight and vision into all that there is: past, present, and future. It reveals the light of the consciousness within.

When meditating upon the third eye, the universe opens up, and as the universe opens, one must open one's mind to the universal maps that lie within oneself. A blocked brow chakra may cause one to have allergies or headaches. One may be unable to feel compassion and empathy for others and may be unduly critical of oneself, seeing the universe as a judge.

When the brow chakra is healthy and balanced, it gives one humor and compassion. It allows one to see the universe clearly and to make sense of what one sees. It helps one to be open and alert, able to see the inner glow that shines in the eyes of others.

The note for the brow chakra is A, its tone is E, its element is light, its instrument is a crystal bowl, and its mantra is ah.

Affirmation: I see my life experience with a spiritual eye.

The Seventh Chakra – The Crown Chakra

The crown chakra is located on the top of the head and is also known as the thousand petal lotus. It is the seat of the soul. Universal information from the higher self flows into one through the crown chakra.

Working with this energy allows knowledge to flow through one, and one becomes more aware of one's surroundings in this world and in the unseen world. It allows one to become one with all that there is: all living creation on earth.

One is never out of balance with the crown chakra as one is always connected to the creator of the universe and to oneself.

One always has the love of one's teachers in spirit, who love unconditionally, and the love of one's higher self, for one is always on one's path spiritually.

The note for the crown chakra is B, its tone is E, its element is all elements, its instrument is the human voice, and its mantra is ohm.

A helpful exercise: Get comfortable either in a chair or lying on the floor; be sure to keep your spine straight. Go into your mind's eye and see your oneness with the creator. Take three deep breaths – then release. Feel your body relax as the oneness comes. Sit quietly and feel the peace that comes.

Affirmation: I am deserving and worthy of the universe's blessings upon me, and I am open to accepting the blessings at this time.

CHAPTER FOUR

THE ANIMAL WITHIN

BOAR

Harmony: Spread the Light

Good Heart – Faith – Friend – Protector

The Boar has it all! Harmony, light, goodness of heart, and faith. Boar is a friend and protector. Do you feel like your life is out of harmony? If so, take time to take care of the little things you have been putting off. Take care of one thing at a time. As you do this, you will feel the harmony of the Boar coming into your life. With the harmony will come the light.

If you look closely through the fog, you will see the sun shining brightly. So, start to take care of the little things that will bring you a peaceful heart. As your heart fills with light, you will be able to extend your heart to yourself and to others. They will feel the light of a peaceful heart. As the light of a peaceful heart fills you, the faith to accomplish bigger things will come much more easily. For you have the faith. Boar is saying, "Keep your faith strong, and it will all come to pass."

Do you need to be a friend to yourself, to share your own light with yourself, and find the harmony within your heart to have faith? Is there a friend that you can hold out your hand to so they can feel the joy? Are you being too open with your feelings? Boar is the protector. Be careful with what you share, and with whom. Are you aware of an injustice being done to a friend, or to yourself? Do you need to be a protector for a friend, or for yourself?

Remember, start by taking care of the little things you have been putting off. To receive harmony, light, and peacefulness of heart, be a friend to yourself and others. It may be as simple as holding out your hand and saying hello. Boar is bringing you faith today.

CRANE

Balance – Poise – Strength – Creativity – Security

The Crane has beauty and grace when in motion and when standing still. There is a heavenly feeling with the Crane. Do you think a Crane could ever win against a tiger?

Once there was a mother Crane that had three baby Cranes. They were well hidden in the reeds of the lake. It was a bright and beautiful day, and they were enjoying the warmth of the sun when, all of a sudden, a tiger popped its head through the reeds.

"Well," the tiger thinks, "here is an easy meal!"

But the tiger underestimated the mother Crane and was surprised when she stood her ground. She was protecting what she believed in. With poise and balance, the mother Crane began to jump around and strike at the tiger. You may ask what the Crane could strike at the tiger with - her wings! The mother Crane hopped, and flapped, and struck all around the tiger with her wings. The startled and confused tiger struggled to evade her. The peaceful Crane used her creativity and strength to defend herself and her family. Soon, the tiger got tired and decided the Crane was too much trouble. The mother Crane, using what she knows: balance, strength, creativity and poise, was able to defeat the tiger, and overcome the obstacle.

Try standing on one leg as Crane does for a minute or two. You will find it takes strength, poise, and confidence to do so. As you do this, you will open up to your higher self. Is your life out of balance? Do you need a little more poise in your life? Ask Crane to help you find what you need. Is there a tiger around you? If so, use your creativity, and you will find that the tiger will soon leave.

DOG

Faith – Friend – Justice – Loyalty – Time to Play

How long has it been since you have howled at the moon? Go ahead and howl! Have you been working too hard at your job, around the house, or even in your relationship with your mate? It's time to play! Let life in - it's been a while since you have done so. Now is the time to do it. Play!

Dog is a very loyal friend and knows the true meaning of unconditional love. Are you being a loyal and true friend to yourself? Is there a friend in need of your help? Is someone asking you to do something not true to your own nature? Stay true to yourself.

Dog has a great deal of faith. Dog knows there will always be food to eat, someone to love or to play with, and someone to share loyalty and friendship with. Dog has a great sense of justice. Dog knows right from wrong. Dog knows the justice of doing the right thing. It may not be the easy way, but it is the right way. Is someone not being a good friend by being disloyal to you? Has someone hurt you? Dog is saying to ask for justice for all and seek the best for all concerned, including yourself. Dog is saying to howl at the moon, for you have a true friend with you today.

So, go ahead and howl with everything you are!

DRAGON

The Mystical One from the Stars Above

Heart – Light – Encompassing Power – Energy – Challenges

The Dragon is with you today. You are truly blessed, for it will be a magical day. Dragon is magical, and comes into your life from the stars above. Have you ever wondered what it would be like to come face-to-face with a fire breathing Dragon and live to tell of your adventures with the magical one? What a wonderful gift the heavens above have opened up to you.

Is there something or someone you have been wishing would come into your life? Is there a prayer that you have been holding close to your heart? Well, look to the stars and into the heavens, for there you will find Dragon and the answers that are right for you.

Dragon is pure of heart, and its light shines brightly. Speak what is in your heart, and let your own light shine through. Dragon has great power, and all the energy you'll require to meet every challenge ahead of you. If your energy field is low, sit for a few minutes and ask Dragon to come face-to-face with you.

Feel Dragon's energy being given to you. Give thanks, for you are receiving the all encompassing power of the Dragon. Do you have a challenge that needs to be dealt with today? Don't worry about it; you have the purity of heart and light and the encompassing power and energy of the Dragon to help with any task that may lie before you.

EAGLE

Take Flight - Lost Child Within - Overview of All – Spirituality

hy does the Eagle soar high in the sky? Because the Eagle can!

Eagle's eyes are sharp and can see any movement on the ground. Is there a problem that you are not seeing clearly? Well, do not worry, Eagle is lending its eyes to you. Feel the wind beneath your wings. Lift your sights up. The Eagle builds its nest high on mountain tops. Eagle has an overview of all.

Have you lost the child within you? Have you lost the ability to feel the joy, or see the wonder of something old, or new, and to see it as a child would see it for the first time? Look with childlike eyes and see the light, joy, and freedom of the flight that lies within. Look into the mirror and remember the lost child within. Set your spirit free! Ask the Eagle to come in when you are doing your meditation, saying prayers for someone, or praying for yourself. There is no need to walk on the ground all the time. So take flight!

Is there a book you have been putting off reading? Eagle is saying to look at your spirituality. Is there something holding you back, or is it you holding yourself back? Your wings are not clipped, so take flight. Why does the Eagle soar so high in the sky? Simply because it can. So can you!

GRASSHOPPER

Mobility – Hunches – Good Cheer – Inner Voice

The Grasshopper! What a wonderful example to have for today. Today is going to be a great day for you. Listen closely to your inner voice today; follow through on a hunch. Your inner voice may be telling you to put a trip on hold, or to stay at home and rest. Perhaps it is time to fulfill a contract with yourself, or with someone else.

You may ask yourself, 'What does my inner voice sound like?'

Your inner voice is a hunch that you feel within. Imagine you are beginning a project and you think to yourself, 'I may need six of these items, but you don't listen to your instinct, or hunch, and you only get four items. Later, when you are short of what you need to complete your project, you ask yourself, 'Why didn't I listen to my hunch and get six?'

Grasshopper is saying, 'Listen to your hunches and you will not jump in the wrong direction. Grasshopper is bringing good cheer today, so, be happy! Something unexpected is going to happen to you today. It will put a smile on your face and good cheer in your heart. You will be surprised at the results you get when you listen to your inner voice.

 Have you ever watched a Grasshopper jump? Grasshoppers never jump backward; they always jump forward. A Grasshopper is able to leap ten times its own height. So jump forward and do not look back. Jump for the stars! You have the ability to do so.

HORSE

Wind - Vision – Light – Freedom

Is there a vision that you have been holding close to you? Do you feel that a change is coming in your life?

The Horse is a magnificent animal; be ready for some wonderful insight into your life today. It is your time to run free with no fear of what is going on. It is time to take a journey into your vision and into a change that you have asked for! You may have already had this vision.

Do you feel a strong urge to change something in your life? With change will come freedom. Do you keep quiet the words you hold in your heart, words you know to be true? Let the words come from your heart to your mouth; feel your freedom as you speak your truth! There is no need to be locked into one's self anymore. Jump the fence that holds you within! Feel the wind in your face, release the weight of your body, and let Horse carry you.

Walk into your vision, your freedom, and into the light that you hold within yourself. Where there was once darkness, there will be light for you. Green fields are just ahead of you, so do not worry about the changes before you, for these changes need to come about for the fence to be taken down.

Have the faith to ride forward whenever you feel tired. Feel the energy of the Horse and visualize yourself climbing onto its back and moving forward into your truth, into the light, and into a new freedom of self; the higher self. Horse will carry you into your vision.

LEOPARD

Developing Trust - Limits - Learning Quickly – Sexuality

The Leopard is about developing trust. You may be asking, "Do I need to trust in other people, or in myself?" Go within and look at yourself. Is there a decision at hand or a move of some kind of which you are unsure? Trust yourself. It is all about you, and that's okay!

Regarding your sexuality, do you feel your male or female energies are out of balance? Do you need to take some time to bring your energies back into balance? Maybe you need to do a ten or fifteen minute meditation? Are you being too hard on yourself? If so, be kind to yourself; go within to find out if it's the female or male energy that is out of balance. Learn to nurture yourself.

Perhaps there is too much female energy around you. If so, let a little male energy in. Look for the balance that works for you. There will be something that you will learn quickly. It could be something that you will read and everything will fall into place, or you will see something, or someone will say a word to you that makes sense. So Leopard is telling you to keep your ears and eyes open. A piece of the puzzle will fall into place today, so trust yourself when you find it.

Leopard is about taking great leaps. If you have the trust within yourself to take it, there really is nothing to worry about, for the Leopard is leaping with you. If you're not sure of your own limits, ask Leopard to help you to bring in the balance of your energies to help you with the inner you. You are asking yourself to trust yourself. Find your balance! Know your limits. Have trust in the higher self. And give thanks for that great leap you are about to take.

LOTUS

Purity - Breath of Life - Consciousness - Blossoming

The Lotus is the purist of the flowers. The petals of the flower are ready to blossom for you today. Go out and smell the flowers that are in your life right now, or you may want to go out and buy flowers. Watch as each petal unfolds. Look at the purity of the flower, the simplicity, the light and the love that are being given to you right now.

Take a moment to breathe in the beauty and the wonderful scent of the flower. Let your petals unfold within you.

The Lotus has come to you with the breath of life today. Breathe in deeply; feel the breath of life all the way down to your stomach. Be aware of your breath. When was the last time you listened to your own breathing? Do you take short breaths? Do you breathe quickly, or slowly? Try inhaling for the count of three, and then exhaling for the count of three.

Lotus is asking you to repeat this a few times. Feel your energy returning to you. Be aware that your consciousness has awakened within you. Is someone trying to talk you out of something? Be aware of your new awareness, and know that you have the answer within you already.

You can use your new awareness to go within to find all the answers you seek. As you look within, the petals of the flower open, and each petal in your life is unfolded. Your consciousness has opened up to a new way of living. Many things will start to unfold for you now. It may be that a new job or relationship is waiting for you. You will have the awareness to see the true beauty of yourself as it unfolds.

What a wonderful gift it is to be aware of this blossoming within. Lotus is bringing you divine love today. As you go through your day feel the love that has been given to you. Stop from time-to-time to feel the love and warmth from the universe that surrounds you. Share this gift of awareness with other people, perhaps by simply offering a kind word or a helping hand. You'll find that something as small as a smile will brighten their day as well as yours.

MONKEY

Flexibility – Accomplishments – Tasks - Child's Eye

The Monkey sways from branch to branch, twisting and turning in every direction with the greatest of ease. Monkey can see with a child's eye the playfulness, wonderfulness, and the newness of every task at hand. Monkey is flexible while doing the task that is in front of it. Monkey looks at its accomplishments as a child would - with pride and joy. Is it time to take the starch out of this shirt? Is there something on which you can be a little more flexible?

There are many vines to travel to get to the treetops. Swing from one vine to the next to reach your goal. Is there a task at hand that you have been putting off for one reason or another?

Well, Monkey is saying to stop, have a banana, and consider how you might have fun with it. See with a child's eye and imagine what fun you can have with this task. Joke about the task at hand; make a game out of it! Monkey is saying that when all is done, you should look at what you have accomplished and realize the way you accomplished it was by being flexible.

Have fun! See with a child's eye. Be proud of yourself. You have made it to the tree tops, so enjoy the view from up there. And have another banana for a task well done!

OX

Truth - Natural Laws - Opportunities – Abundance

You may be thinking, "Oh no, I've have been drawn to the Ox today! What could the Ox have to offer me today?" Well, let's take a look at one's truth and see what Ox will be bringing you today. The Ox pulls the plow straight. Are you staying true to your course? Have you forgotten the truth that lies beneath your feet? Is it truth that lives underfoot, or an illusion?

You know the truth of your path, so honor this truth in yourself and start to plow your field, and as you do, the opportunities and abundance will start to grow. You need to take a look at your path. You have the inner strength. Ask yourself what natural laws you have forgotten? Is it working in your yard to reconnect with the energies of mother earth, or sitting quietly to be a little more grounded?

Honor this time with spirit as it is honoring this day with you. What opportunities are you missing? Are you looking all around you instead of recognizing the abundance and opportunities that are right in front of you? Ox is saying that all your opportunities, abundance, and truth are right in front of you.

Whether it has to do with family, friends, or a lover, stop looking up or to the side. The answer is right at your feet, next to mother earth. This is a gift the Ox brings to you today.

PHOENIX

Journey – Warrior – Rising Above – Rebirth

The Phoenix has come into your life today, so hold on tight! Get ready for a powerful journey, be it one of body, mind, or soul. Phoenix is very powerful. Have you been asking for a journey? What you have been asking for will come to you on the wings of Phoenix. Phoenix is also a warrior.

Phoenix is a protector of all. So, be brave and ride on the wings of Phoenix, for this is a journey you have been asking for. Do you feel that someone is keeping you from starting, or completing, your journey, or that you have stood in your own way, just look down and you will find you are on the shoulder of Phoenix, ready to take flight.

Remember, Phoenix is very powerful and mighty, and will lift you above all that stands in your way. You can rise above it all. You have the wisdom within you.

Therefore, go on your journey! And like Phoenix, you will rise up through the ashes of the fire, shining brightly and unharmed! It is your time for a rebirth.

Maybe this is your journey to a wonderful, new, and exciting time as you let go of the old. Ride on the shoulders of Phoenix, up through the ashes of the fire, unharmed, shining brightly into a new rebirth of who you truly are: A bright shining soul in the heavens of the universe!

RABBIT

Energies – Future – Commitment – Decision – Success

What is being asked of you is that you look at your fears. The Rabbit is furry, lovable, and cuddly. Have you ever taken the time to study the movements of the Rabbit?

The Rabbit will sit there and appear to be twitching; it may look like it is afraid of something. What the Rabbit is doing is feeling the energy all around it. Suddenly, it makes a decision and takes off in a flash.

Fear comes in many forms. Today is the day to look at what your fears are. Fear of the future? Of not knowing what life holds for you? Take a moment to look back at your life. See the actions you have taken and where they have brought you, then apply this knowledge to the future. If you like what you see, great! If not, make a decision to change it until you see the future you desire.

Do you have a fear of commitment to yourself, a mate, your health, or maybe even work? Are you ready to make that commitment, or is fear stopping you? What price are you willing to pay for the success you want?

You can start with the small things. Make a decision, a commitment to follow through on what you have asked for today. Once you have made that decision your fears will hop away and you will see the green fields that lie ahead of you. MAKE THAT COMMITMENT! Commit to yourself, your higher self, for success. Chase away the fear.

What is fear? It is the unknown, but once it is known it is no longer fear. So sit down and have a carrot! Enjoy the green fields that are all around you.

RAT

Cleaning House - Storing – Family – Friends – Adaptability

The Rat is a clever animal. It is very adaptable to any given location and can survive in the city or the country. Is it time to start cleaning house? Are there things that you have been holding on to that no longer serve you in your life? Have you achieved a new level of learning? It's time to let go of old habits or old friends.

Rat is saying to take off your blinders and look at your growth. See how far you have come. See the new friends that are around you, or is it time to go out and make new friends? Is there a situation so unbelievable that you feel you can not make it through it? Nothing lasts forever; you will survive, so learn to adapt.

Stop looking at what does not work in your life, and start figuring out what does works for you. Step up to the challenge and the new level of awareness that lies before you. Take off the blinders and look at the wonder all around you. Shed the ropes with which you have bound yourself, and behold the beautiful soul you see. It is you!

ROOSTER

Messenger - Survivor – Stamina - Money Collector

The Rooster is a messenger. It is said that if a Rooster comes onto the porch and turns its head to the right and crows, there will be a death of some sort. If the Rooster crows into the house, then you will be sure to have good luck. You may say to yourself, "Well, I don't have a rooster. How can I know what will occur?"

The Rooster is a messenger of tidings. The 'death' you may experience today may mean giving up something that no longer serves you. Perhaps some not-so-nice thoughts toward other people. It may be time to replace them with kinder, gentler thoughts.

The Rooster is crowing straight into your soul - be ready for good things to happen today! You are a survivor. You have survived many things during your lifetime. Is there something going on in your life right now that has you wondering if you will survive?

Rooster is here to let you know you will survive to see another sunrise. Look for a feather to let you know Rooster is near you today. The Rooster is bringing you stamina today, so, if you feel tired take three deep breaths and walk out into the yard knowing that Rooster by your side. You will have all the stamina and energy you need to complete the task at hand. The task may involve a collection of some kind. Have you been putting off collecting some money that is owed to you? Or have you put off collecting something that you loaned to someone else?

Rooster will give you all the stamina and energy you need to accomplish your task. Open your hands and your pockets, for money is coming to you. Strut proudly, for you have the Rooster by your side.

SHEEP

Creative - Kind Hearted – You Have Come Home – Optimistic

The Sheep has come to you today. Sheep is kind hearted, gentle, and has great strength. True strength comes from gentleness. Sheep was there when one of the great masters was born. As each day brings a new birth, Sheep brings you creativity. Today will be an excellent day to use your imagination to create something new in your life. No matter how small it is, create something new in your life, for it will fall into the next day. Be kind hearted today; be gentle with yourself and others.

You may have a task today that you feel may take some harshness to handle. Sheep is asking you to remember that you can create what you want with a gentle action and a kind heart.

Sheep is also asking you to come home today, to be one with yourself. Maybe today is the day to create the oneness within. Go within and search for the oneness that you seek. Follow the inner self of who you are, not what you think you are. Be optimistic for today. Look for the opportunity that lies at your feet. What you search for is right there.

You may be telling yourself that it will never work, but remember, you have Sheep with you today. Be optimistic about it. You may be surprised at what happens. Watch your thoughts, watch your words, and watch your actions. You will create it. You may be planning to buy something today.

Sheep has come to ask you to be careful not to overspend. Are you looking for the best buys, or are you overextending yourself? Either way, Sheep says to be careful for today.

SNAKE

Warmth – Rebirth - Forgiveness – Health – Healing – Sexuality

The Snake has come to you today. You may be thinking to yourself, "That slimy thing!" Or you may have some other ideas about the Snake. Let's see if we can develop some different thought patterns about the Snake. Snake is a wonderful healer. In the medical world there are two Snakes that meet one another. It is the medical insignia known all over the world for health and healing. If we do not have our health, what do we have?

So, when the Snake comes to you, it is asking you to take a look at your health. Are you smoking too much, over eating, or not eating foods that are right for you? Are you in poor health right now, or waiting for your prayers to be answered? Whichever it may be, Snake has come to you with health and healing.

Snake may be suggesting that you shed the old and come into the rebirth. Ask yourself, "Is it time to shed the old?" Snake is saying to go within; you have the answers within you. Come out of the cold and into the warmth of the sun.

Lie on the warm grass or in a nice warm place. Or lie in your yard, as the Snake does, to soak up the healing energies of the sun and of mother earth. The Snake is a sign of forgiveness. Snake is asking you to forgive yourself and others. Let your health and healing begin now. Snake is about learning difficult lessons, and Snake is here to help you with those lessons. You have it within you to rise above them all! If the Snake comes to you in a dream, put a smile on your face, for there may be a lover or new relationships coming to you soon. Snake is bringing you health and healing.

TIGER

Courageous - Powerful - Loving – Achievement

Courageous and powerful, Tiger is loving of all life. As a Tiger walks through the night, its eyes shine and the other animals honor its presence. A Tiger is well grounded; it knows its territory. A Tiger's roar can be heard from afar. It sometimes goes where others dare not go.

If Tiger has come into your life, there are four different things it wishes you to look at:

One: Tiger is asking you to be courageous as you attend to a task at hand or a decision that needs to be made. Draw upon the courageous power of Tiger.

Two: Is your power low and you need more energy? Perhaps a little cat-nap would be refreshing. Fifteen minutes or so is all one really needs to awaken the power of the sleeping Tiger within. Listen to the powerful roar of the Tiger within.

Three: Tigers are very loving and protective of their cubs while they are young. Tiger is very loving toward itself, and Tiger may be asking you to be kind and loving to yourself. Are you showing your claws to your mate, family, friends, or even yourself? You can have the Tiger within you and still be loving and caring.

Four: Whenever a Tiger makes its kill for dinner, it lies down next to it as if to say, "Look what I have achieved!" Tiger may be asking you to be proud of your achievements. Whether it has to do with work that went unnoticed, or a household task you did for your family or friends, Tiger is encouraging you to show your achievements.

You have drawn Tiger, so put the sparkle back in your eyes. For you have something to roar about.

CHAPTER FIVE

THE ELEMENTS

MOTHER EARTH

Energy – Wisdom – Patience - Prosperity

Are you ready to learn from Mother Earth? She uses much energy to help us grow. Have you ever stopped to consider what these energies are? Let's look at some of them. She is found in the trees and plants all around us. The greenery supplies us with the air that we breathe. Where does the energy come from? From Mother Earth, and she offers these energies to you today. Go outside and stand or sit on the ground and feel her energies come into you.

Visualize negative energy flowing down the right side of you into Mother Earth, and then feel the healing energy flowing up into you through your left side. Do this for five or ten minutes. Keep the circle of these energies going until you feel reenergized, and give thanks to Mother Earth for a wonderful healing through the energies that she gives so freely. Is there a question on your mind today? Be assured that you will get the answer from Mother Earth.

You are being asking to look a little deeper; ask yourself what you have learned from both your question and the answer that has been given to you. Maybe it has to do with patience. Mother Earth may be asking you not to make a hasty decision, to have some patience and let things unfold as they will in their own time. Perhaps you need to be a little more patient with yourself.

There are no mistakes; you are doing what you are supposed to be doing, when you are doing it. This is how you grow and learn.

There is prosperity for you today. It is for you to see where this prosperity has come in your life. Within every acorn is the seed of a mighty oak tree. Everything the acorn needs to become a mighty oak lives within its small shell.

When the acorn falls to the ground, the energies of Mother Earth help it to become a mighty oak. Therefore, it is within you to become a magnificent being.

WATER

Flexibility – Awareness – Intuition – New Ideas – Fullness

Water is a peaceful medium. Water has many strengths. Have you ever stopped to recognize how versatile Water is? Water can move mountains or hold something in place. Water can be hot or cold and still hold its power and strength. Water can heal your body and your soul. Water gives nourishment to your body.

Have you ever thrown a pebble into a pond and watched the ripples it creates? Perhaps you have nudged a glass of Water and seen the ripples on the surface. Water may be asking, "Have you just thrown a pebble into the Waters of life?" Once you are conscious of your thoughts you become aware of the power you hold within you. The ripples of life come back to you ten times as fast as the ripples of your thoughts or actions went out. Your awareness has come alive within.

So be careful; you can manifest anything you want in the blink of an eye, whether it is positive or negative. Water may be suggesting that you go with the flow. As a leaf floats down the river it may run into a log or rock. The leaf does not fight the obstacle in front of it; the leaf allows the Water to gently carry it around the obstacle.

Use the energy of the Water so you can float easily down the river of life. How about a bath this morning, or this evening? Submerge your whole body in the Waters of life. Feel the healing energies that come to you from Water. This awareness is the gift of Water. The flow of your life has begun.

FIRE

Leadership – Positive – Motivation- Good Listener

Fire is telling you that it is time to take the lead! Be a teacher. Is there something or someone that you have been standing behind? If so, today is a good day to show your leadership.

Take a chance. Who knows, you may enjoy being the leader. Show your leadership. You have the Fire within, so, get ready to be motivated! Feel the Fire lighting up within you, and let the Fire spread to your body, mind, and soul. Remember that you do not need to take giant steps; one foot in front of the other will get you there just as fast.

What you do today will carry you into tomorrow. Be positive, do not doubt yourself. Listen to the Fire deep within. There is no room for doubt or failure. Know what you are feeling, and trust your inner self.

Have you ever watched a campfire, or perhaps watched a fireplace at home? See how the Fire dances around! You may see a vision. Listen to the Fire. It could be asking you to listen to yourself and to others around you.

 Listen to what is being said. Fire is saying, "Remember, leaders are not born, they are made." Stay motivated and be positive in the task you are doing. Listen, and then show the leader that dwells within you. Fire is saying, "Go out and spread your warmth to yourself and others."

METAL

Independent Impulses - Own - Way Wisdom - Plum Blossom

With the Metal card you will experience independence. It's time for you to step out. Have you been holding on to someone, or to a group consciousness? One of the lessons with Metal is that we come into this world alone, and we leave alone. During our life span we learn independence. Is there someone, or some group, you need to release? If so, bless them and let go. This does not mean you no will longer speak to them. It just means it is time for you to go to a new level. It's like learning a profession.

At first you need a teacher. Then, as you learn your job, you no longer need that teacher; you know how to do the job. Metal is saying, "You'll make progress in achieving a oneness with your higher self." You may have to watch your impulses today, because with Metal comes impulsiveness. Have you ever done something on impulse and thought to yourself, "Why didn't I think this through?"

 Think about a decision you need to make today. Take the time to choose the right path for yourself, and watch out for that impulse that comes to you. Be careful with your energies. They will be very strong, and you will be able to influence the people around you. You may even try to get your own way! But in doing that, you will interfere with their choice or free will. You will have an awareness of what is happening; but they may not understand, so use the wisdom of your higher self to be aware of that difference in perception.

With this wisdom you will know how to use the gifts given to you.

WOOD

Adapts – Produces – Rewards – Sharing - Peony

Wood has come into your life today. Mother Nature has brought you a great gift. Have you ever stopped to look at a tree blowing in a strong wind? You will see the tree swaying back and forth in harmony with the wind. The branches bend, but they do not break. And the ones that do break are dry and brittle, with no give to them.

The tree knows what kind of tree it is and is happy with that. No matter what kind of energy is thrown at the tree, the tree will adapt to it. When the day is done, the tree will be standing tall because of its ability to adapt to whatever force it had to face. The lesson with wood is to learn to adapt to what lies in front of you.

As you learn to adapt to different things, you will begin to produce the sweet fruit of the tree of life. Wood is asking, "Is there a strong wind blowing your way?" If so, do not run…accept the energies, adapt to what is coming to you. Know who you are, as the tree does.

 Wood is by your side. Gaze in wonder at what you have produced from the tree of life. The rewards will be many. Wood is asking you to remember to share your good fortune with others, whether it is with a helping hand or just a smile. By doing so, you water your tree of life. For, you see, Wood and Water go hand in hand. As you are out and about today, look for the peony. The peony flower is associated with Wood and love.

YIN

Female - Soft - Time - Probably Receptive

The Yin has come into your life for a very good reason today. It represents your feminine side, which is in all of us whether we are male or female.

Is it time to lighten up on yourself, or on something in your life that you have been hard on yourself about? If so, be kind to yourself. More than likely you are able to show the soft side of yourself to family and friends, even strangers. So why not share the softness with yourself? Or maybe you are being too hard on your mate, children, or friends. If so, Yin is saying to you, "Stop it!"

Take a little time to meditate on the task at hand. Are you being hard on them because it is about them, or is it really about you? Yin, or the universe, is teaching you a lesson. It is time to let the softness and gentleness into your life, and as you do you will find yourself at peace in no time at all.

The task at hand will be clear. Yin is showing you that you're entering the Valley. You may be thinking, "Oh no, what now?" Not to worry, the Valley is a wonderful place. You will find a great gift is brought to you by Yin. Since you have drawn the Yin you will be receptive to this wonderful gift.

Above all, Yin would like to let you know that now is time to go to the Valley and look for the softness. Find the female side and the gentleness that dwells within you. The Valley is inside of you. Here is where you will find the gift of Yin.

YANG

Male – Mountain – Sun – Fire – Active – Outdoors

The Yang Card has shown up! It is time to show your inner strength. Yang is the opposite of the Yin. Yang is saying to you, "It's time to tap into your male energy." Have you been seeking a change in your life, but keep putting it off? Well, now is the time to take a stand. Go into meditation and ask the universe to show you how to tap into the Yang. It is your time to climb to the top of the mountain.

You may find rocks or brush in your way, or you may have to make your own road up the mountain. Either way, do not worry; Yang and the universe are here to help clear the pathway for you. When you find an obstacle in your way as you go up the mountain, don't rush around it. Stop for a moment and remove the obstacle so the way will be clear both going up and coming back down. Maybe you have reached the top of your mountain.

Yang has come to you today to let you know you have arrived! Yang also stands for Fire. Maybe you need to get fired up so you can start to move on what is going on in your life. Or, it could be Yang has come to let you know you need some warmth in your life. Are you being cold to yourself, or someone else? If so, Yang is saying, "Show some love and warmth; you may be surprised at what will happen!"

Fire is also representative of the color red. Maybe you need to wear something red today or add some red to your diet. This day is about being active, so get out and about. It's a good day to take care of what needs to be done. You have drawn the Yang Card, so don't put anything off today. Yang is about the outdoors and sunshine. Today is not a good day to sit inside. Yang is saying, "Get outside and be active!" Climb your mountain. Enjoy life. Soak up the sun ~ the life giving energy of the Yang.

YIN & YANG

Balance - Seeds - Creative Energy - Reality

Yin and Yang, the creativity of your life, is saying to you, "Make a list of the things that contribute to how wonderful you are feeling today."

You have drawn the card of balance: Yin and Yang. Take a moment to breathe in the balance and relax; the balance will flow into you. Is there a task at which you have been working that you feel is out of balance? Or are you just feeling out of balance with life? If so, rest assured, today is the day the task, or your life, will come into balance.

Today is a time to plant the seeds of your future. You have come full circle with yourself, you have prepared the garden of your soul, and today is a day to plant the seeds of creativity and energy.

With the Yin and Yang comes creative energy. There are things that are wonderful and positive that will work in your life right now. You have the balance and creative energies within you. By making your list you are planting seeds in the garden. Plant the seeds of your creativity and energy, and then watch your garden grow.

The balance will be there more and more for you. Yin and Yang is also asking you to be aware of your reality. What is it that works for you right now? There are two sides to the Yin and Yang: black and white, positive and negative. Remember, your reality may not be someone else's, and his or her reality may not be yours.

This is how you will find the balance of the Yin and Yang in your garden of life.